Project Learning Through American History

CONSIDERING DIFFERENT OPINIONS SURROUNDING

THE AMERICAN REVOLUTIONARY WAR

FLETCHER C. FINCH

PowerKiDS press™

NEW YORK

Published in 2019 by The Rosen Publishing Group, Inc.
29 East 21st Street, New York, NY 10010

Editor: Therese Shea
Book Design: Rachel Rising

Photo Credits: Cover https://commons.wikimedia.org/wiki/File:Washington_Crossing_the_Delaware_by_Emanuel_Leutze,_MMA-NYC,_1851.jpg; cover, pp. 1, 3, 4, 5, 6, 7, 8, 9, 10, 11, 12, 14, 15, 16, 18, 20, 22, 23, 24, 25, 26, 28, 29, 30, 31, 32 (background) Lyubov_Nazarova/Shutterstock.com; pp. 4, 6, 8, 10, 12, 20, 24, 28 (insert) kontur-vid/Shutterstock.com; pp. 5, 9, 11, 13, 15, 19 Courtesy of the Library of Congress; p. 7 https://commons.wikimedia.org/wiki/File:Benjamin_Franklin_1767.jpg; p. 14 https://commons.wikimedia.org/wiki/File:Boston_Tea_Party-1973_issue-3c.jpg; p. 17 https://commons.wikimedia.org/wiki/File:Flickr_-_USCapitol_-_The_First_Continental_Congress,_1774.jpg; p. 21 https://commons.wikimedia.org/wiki/File:Philip_Dawe_(attributed),_The_Bostonians_Paying_the_Exciseman,_or_Tarring_and_Feathering_(1774).jpg; p. 22 https://commons.wikimedia.org/wiki/File:RossBetsy.jpg; p. 23 https://commons.wikimedia.org/wiki/File:Salomon,_Haym_(bust)_-_NARA_-_532941.jpg; p. 25 Louis S. Glanzman/National Geographic/Getty Images; p. 27 SuperStock/SuperStock/Getty Images; p. 29 https://commons.wikimedia.org/wiki/File:Soldiers_of_the_Continental_Army.gif; p. 30 https://commons.wikimedia.org/wiki/File:Surrender_of_Lord_Cornwallis.jpg.

Cataloging-in-Publication Data

Names: Finch, Fletcher C.
Title: Considering different opinions surrounding the American Revolutionary War / Fletcher C. Finch
Description: New York : PowerKids Press, 2019. | Series: Project learning through American history | Includes glossary and index.
Identifiers: LCCN ISBN 9781538330562 (pbk.) | ISBN 9781538330555 (library bound) | ISBN 9781538330579 (6 pack)
Subjects: LCSH: United States--History--Revolution, 1775-1783--Juvenile literature.
Classification: LCC E208.F56 2019 | DDC 973.3--dc23

Manufactured in the United States of America

CPSIA Compliance Information: Batch #CS18PK For further information contact Rosen Publishing, New York, New York at 1-800-237-9932.

CONTENTS

FROM 13 COLONIES TO ONE NATION

In the 17th and 18th centuries, England created colonies in the eastern part of North America. These colonies didn't form one organized group. They were separate colonies, started at different times by different people. Each colony had its own local government that decided most laws, but all were considered part of England.

Over time, the colonies became more closely connected to each other. Many colonists started to think that England, all the way across the Atlantic Ocean, shouldn't have so much power over them. Unpopular taxes and laws angered many.

Considering Different Opinions

As you read about people involved in the American Revolutionary War, think about the opinions they held. Their opinions were shaped by where they lived, their role in society, their jobs, and their families. The experiences they had, the people they knew, and the things they read also helped form their opinions. Considering the roots of people's opinions will help you understand more about the American Revolution's causes.

Benjamin Franklin first printed this cartoon in 1754, encouraging American colonies to join forces against France and its Native American **allies** during the French and Indian War (1756–1763). It was printed again during the American Revolution. What do you think was Franklin's opinion regarding the revolution?

JOIN, or DIE.

A **revolution** began in 1775, when the 13 colonies joined together to fight British taxes and laws and then the country of England itself. The colonies declared independence from England in 1776 and soon became the United States of America.

PATRIOT, LOYALIST, OR NEUTRAL

When the American Revolutionary War began, people living in the colonies mostly belonged to three groups: patriots, Loyalists, and those who were neutral, or didn't support either side. Patriots believed that England had been unfair to the colonies and that the colonists needed to fight for their own rights. Loyalists thought of themselves as British citizens and believed **rebellion** was wrong. There were still others who didn't want to be involved in the fighting at all.

A Loyal Prisoner

*William Franklin was a Loyalist who helped England during the American Revolution. He was put in prison by American patriots in 1777. Why would William Franklin have been so loyal to England? Doing **research** into his life can help you understand why he held his opinions. As royal governor of New Jersey, he would have been appointed to his job by the king. Why do you think this made him loyal to the British government?*

Benjamin Franklin (shown here) was a patriot and Founding Father. William Franklin was the royal governor of New Jersey.

The side a person chose depended on what they thought of events before the war and during the fighting. Some people had much to gain or lose from independence. Neighbors and even families were split about the revolution. For example, Benjamin Franklin was a famous patriot, but his son William Franklin was a Loyalist.

TAXATION WITHOUT REPRESENTATION

For most of the 1600s, the British **Parliament** had little to do with the American colonies. By the end of the century, Parliament established some trade laws. Its first tax—on molasses and sugar from the French West Indies—was placed on the colonies in 1733. After the French and Indian War ended in 1763, the British government needed money to support its army in America, so Parliament started to pass new taxes on the colonies.

Research the Right Way

When you're trying to figure out why someone holds an opinion, the best research method is to ask them! However, that doesn't help with people who lived during the American Revolution like John Dickinson. Luckily, Dickinson was an author, so you can find out what he thought by reading his own words. His most famous writings were Letters from a Farmer in Pennsylvania to the Inhabitants of the British Colonies, *which appeared in colonial newspapers.*

In the mid-1700s, U.S. Founding Father John Dickinson wrote that Parliament didn't have a right to tax the colonies and could only make rules about trade. Why would he support some colonial rights but not call for total independence?

If you were a colonist, how would you feel about paying taxes to England? Would you accept the taxes because the British military had defended the colonies in the French and Indian War? Or would you be upset because the colonies didn't have **representatives** in Parliament?

THE STAMP ACT

In 1765, Parliament passed the Stamp Act. The law required that colonists pay a tax on every piece of printed paper, including newspapers, signs, and even playing cards. The tax was represented by a special stamp on these things.

Crowds of people angry about the tax attacked officials who were supposed to sell the stamps. Colonial governments also protested, stating that such taxation without colonial representation in the British government was wrong. Parliament repealed, or canceled, the Stamp Act, but declared that it still had the right to create laws and taxes for the colonies.

Consider the Source

When doing your research about the American Revolution, primary sources are a perfect way to find out what was going on. These are things, like the newspaper on page 11, that were created at the time you're studying. Primary sources also include pieces of art, letters, speeches, photographs, and anything else that provides direct information about the time. Sources that weren't created by people who were there during a time period or event are called secondary sources.

Many colonists got their news from papers. The owner of this newspaper wrote that the Stamp Act was forcing him to stop printing. How would this newspaper help form readers' opinions about the Stamp Act?

ne TIMES are
Dreadful,
Dismal
Doleful
Dolorous, and
DOLLAR-LESS.

of the STAMP

An Emblem of the Effects

O! the fatal Stam

Thursday, October 31, 1765.

THE

NUMB. 1195.

PENNSYLVANIA JOURNAL;

AND

WEEKLY ADVERTISER.

EXPIRING: In Hopes of a Resurrection to LIFE again.

I

AM sorry to be obliged to acquaint my Readers, that as The STAMP-ACT, is fear'd to be obligatory upon us after the First of November ensuing, (the fatal To morrow) the Publisher of this Paper unable to bear the Burthen, has thought it expedient TO STOP awhile, in order to deliberate, whether any Methods can be found to elude the Chains forged for us, and escape the insupportable Slavery, which it is hoped, from the last Representations now made against that Act, may be effected. Mean while, I must earnestly Request every Individual of my Subscribers, many of whom have been long behind Hand, that they would immediately Discharge their respective Arrears that I may be able, not only to support myself during the Interval, but be better prepared to proceed again with this Paper, whenever an opening for that Purpose appears, which I hope will be soon.   WILLIAM BRADFORD

How would colonists who had been upset about the Stamp Act feel about its repeal? The tax they hated was gone, but their lack of representation hadn't changed.

AMERICAN PROTESTS

In 1767, Parliament began to pass the Townshend Acts, which stated the colonies would pay taxes on glass, lead, paint, and tea, things they could only buy from England. Again, the colonists were angered. Most of the taxes were later repealed—with the exception of the tax on tea. Because of unrest and violence, British soldiers were stationed in Boston, Massachusetts, to keep the peace.

On March 5, 1770, a crowd in Boston fought with a group of British soldiers. The soldiers fired their guns, killing five people. The soldiers said they'd been attacked. Patriots claimed the soldiers started the trouble. The event was later called the Boston **Massacre**. How might this name have affected people's opinions about this conflict?

Searching for Sources

Paul Revere's engraving on page 13 is an example of a primary source. Revere lived during this time period and his work tells us about his opinion of this event. Many primary sources that have to do with American history can be found on U.S. government websites. The Library of Congress is the research branch of Congress. Its website is www.loc.gov. You can search for primary and secondary sources on this site.

This image by patriot Paul Revere shows British soldiers shooting into a crowd in Boston. What point of view does the artist show? In what way do you think he was hoping to shape people's opinions?

13

THE COERCIVE ACTS

In 1773, patriots in Boston protested England's tax on tea by throwing a shipment of tea into the harbor. After this "Boston Tea Party," Parliament passed the **Coercive** (or Intolerable) Acts in 1774. The acts closed the port of Boston, replaced elected officials in Massachusetts with officials picked by England, and stated the colonies had to provide housing for soldiers.

The U.S. Postal Service created four stamps honoring the Boston Tea Party in 1973.

Patriots boarded three ships and dumped 342 containers of tea into Boston Harbor to protest the tax on tea. Use what Frederick North said below to consider his opinion about what would happen if Massachusetts wasn't punished for the Boston Tea Party.

Parliament hoped to make an example of Massachusetts and force the colonies to admit that England was in charge. Frederick North, the leader of Parliament, said, "The Americans have tarred and feathered your subjects, plundered [stolen from] your merchants, burnt your ships, denied all obedience to your laws and authority . . . We must risk something; if we do not, all is over."

THE FIRST CONTINENTAL CONGRESS

Colonial leaders were alarmed by the Coercive Acts. Twelve colonies sent representatives to Philadelphia, Pennsylvania, in September 1774 for the First Continental Congress. They worked together on a response to Parliament's actions.

The Continental Congress said that the colonists were loyal to the king, but that Parliament's actions were "unjust, and cruel, as well as **unconstitutional**, and most dangerous and destructive of American rights." Why would the colonists support one part of the British government but oppose another?

The colonies agreed to stop trading with England unless Parliament repealed taxes and laws that "threaten destruction to the lives, liberty, and property of His Majesty's subjects in North America." Instead of buying items from England, the Continental Congress encouraged Americans to make things or do without them.

Patrick Henry told the First Continental Congress, "The Distinctions [differences] between Virginians, Pennsylvanians, New Yorkers and New Englanders, are no more. I am not a Virginian, but an American." What point was he making?

THE FIRST CONTINENTAL CONGRESS · 1774

ARGUMENTS FOR INDEPENDENCE

The First Continental Congress asked King George III to use his power to change the laws and called themselves "your Majesty's faithful subjects." They said that harmony between England and the colonies could still be restored. But others thought that the colonies needed to break away from England.

Reverend Jacob Green of Hanover, New Jersey, wrote that the American colonies needed to be a separate country: "By independency we shall avoid tyranny, and **oppression**. If we submit to British government, we shall be continually cramped [overcrowded] with Governors, and other officers appointed by the crown."

Green said trade and farming would improve with independence and freedom-loving people from all over the world would come to America. Why might Green's description of a better America change the way colonists thought about England?

The war began on April 19, 1775, in Lexington and Concord, Massachusetts, when British soldiers attempted to take away colonists' weapons.

19

KING GEORGE III

King George III didn't respond approvingly to the Continental Congress. When he heard that fighting had begun in Massachusetts, he replied with harsh words. He called the patriots "wicked and desperate persons" who were breaking the law and harming trade. He said the American colonists should remember royal power had protected and supported them and remain loyal to him. King George commanded government and military officers to crush the rebellion. He promised to punish the "traitors" and anyone who helped them.

Language Matters

When reading primary sources, language provides a big clue about the opinions of authors. When King George III called the colonists fighting against him "traitors," it's easy to understand his opinion of the revolution. And when these same colonists called themselves "patriots," you know they viewed the revolution and their actions favorably. How might the king calling the patriots "wicked" affect their opinion of him?

In 1774, patriots attacked royal official John Malcolm in Boston. They covered him with hot tar and feathers and forced him to drink hot tea. How would Loyalists view this attack? How would patriots?

The revolution in the American colonies threatened the power of the British Empire and King George III. England had just fought a costly and demanding war against France. How might that have shaped the way British leaders thought about the rebellion of American patriots?

CALLS FOR PEACE

How might religion **influence** the opinions of colonists? Many Quakers remained neutral during the revolution because their faith and traditions are against violence. After the war began, a Quaker group gathered in Philadelphia, Pennsylvania, to call for peace. The Quakers warned that patriots trying to break away from England were "acting in a proud, selfish spirit" and fighting would lead to "the shedding of innocent blood." They noted the benefits the king and British government had provided in the past.

This 1917 painting shows Betsy Ross (second from left) presenting the U.S. flag to George Washington.

People of many different faiths took part in the revolution. Haym Salomon was a Jewish patriot who was captured twice by the British. He escaped and raised money for the Continental army.

Some patriots didn't trust those who were neutral. They forced Quaker shops to close and broke the windows of Quakers' houses. A few Quakers were even arrested. There were some Quakers who joined the fight against England, though. Among them was Betsy Ross, later credited (mistakenly) with creating the U.S. flag.

REMEMBER THE LADIES

Abigail Adams often wrote to her husband, John Adams, when he was away representing Massachusetts in the Continental Congress. She hoped for the start of a better country. Abigail didn't think it was enough to break away from England, though. She said the new American government needed to protect the rights of women and give them representation.

"I desire you would remember the ladies, and be more generous and favourable to them than your ancestors," she wrote to John in March 1776. "Do not put such unlimited power into the hands of the husbands."

More Places to Research

Besides government websites, you can often find trusted sources of information on websites run by colleges and universities. Some of these places collect letters, artwork, and important papers from the revolutionary time period. Copies and images are often placed online for people to study. Many college and public libraries also offer great resources for research—and librarians are experts at knowing where to find the facts you seek!

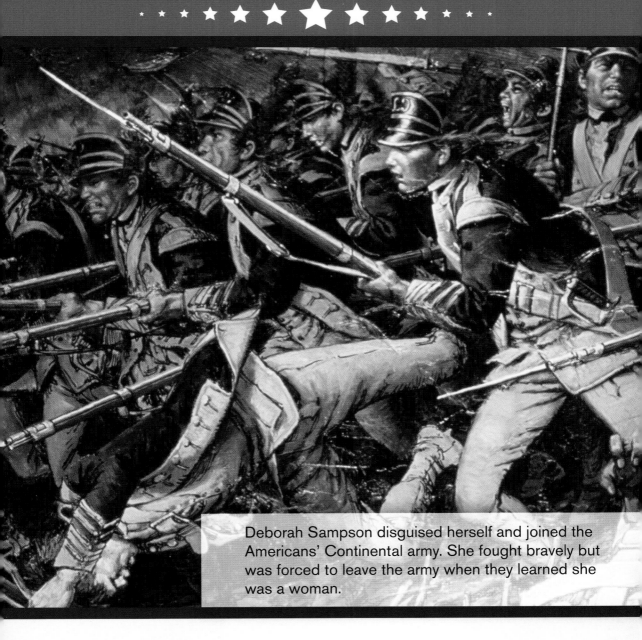

Deborah Sampson disguised herself and joined the Americans' Continental army. She fought bravely but was forced to leave the army when they learned she was a woman.

Research the rights of women at this time and the roles women played. How would these conditions have shaped Abigail's thoughts on government?

NATIVE AMERICANS DIVIDED

Before the Revolution, colonists often fought with Native Americans over land. When the war began, both the British and Americans offered to protect Native American lands if the nations helped them.

The Mohawks sided with the British. Thayendanegea, also called Joseph Brant, was a Mohawk leader. He traveled to England and met with King George III in 1776. "The disturbances in America give great trouble to all our nations," Thayendanegea later said. He added that Mohawks "have on all occasions shown their zeal and loyalty to the great king; yet they have been very badly treated by the people in that country." He asked for fair treatment by England.

Other Native Americans fought alongside the patriots. How would you decide between two sides if you couldn't trust either?

The Haudenosaunee, sometimes called the Iroquois Confederacy, included the Mohawk, Seneca, Onondaga, Oneida, Cayuga, and Tuscarora peoples. They worked together for years, but were divided during the war. Mohawk leader Thayendanegea (Joseph Brant) is shown here.

SEEKING FREEDOM

Free and enslaved African Americans fought on both sides of the American Revolutionary War. African Americans were part of the patriot forces in early battles, and some were honored for bravery.

In 1775, the Virginia Loyalist governor Lord Dunmore offered freedom to any slave who would fight for the British. At first, George Washington didn't want African Americans in the Continental army. As the war continued, though, the Americans also chose to offer freedom to slaves who would fight.

The Opinions of Outsiders

Many patriot leaders were educated men with wealth and land. Some, such as Thomas Jefferson, wrote and spoke about the importance of freedom but owned slaves. Research how people who lived in America but didn't have power—such as slaves, Native Americans, and women—were treated after the war. What might have been their opinion about the new government because of this treatment?

A French officer drew this picture showing members of the Continental army, including an African American soldier. What might African American soldiers have hoped to accomplish by joining the army?

Boyrereau Brinch was a slave in Connecticut who joined the Continental army. Though he himself wasn't free, he fought for the freedom of those who enslaved him. "Alas! Poor African Slave, to liberate freemen, my tyrants," he said. After the war, he was given his freedom.

CONTINUING QUESTIONS

In the 1700s, colonial Americans struggled with deciding what role the British government should have in their lives. After forming their own nation, the Founding Fathers still argued about how to shape their new government.

Even today, Americans have different opinions about the role of the government. They ask questions such as: What is a government's responsibility to its people? Who should make laws? When is freedom more important than safety?

Choose one of these questions or another you have about the role of government. Do some research to find out real opinions about the topic both during the American Revolution and today. Present your answers (and your own opinions!) in a fun and creative way.

On October 19, 1781, British soldiers at Yorktown, Virginia, **surrendered** to the Continental army and its French allies, ending the last major battle of the war.

GLOSSARY

ally: A country that supports and helps another country in a war.

coercive: Using force or threats to make someone do something.

influence: To affect or change in an indirect but usually important way.

massacre: The violent killing of many people.

oppression: Unjust or cruel exercise of authority or power.

Parliament: The British lawmaking body.

rebellion: An effort by many people to change the government or leader of a country by the use of protest or violence.

representative: A member of a lawmaking body who acts for voters.

research: To study something carefully.

revolution: The usually violent attempt by many people to end the rule of one government and start a new one.

surrender: To agree to stop fighting because you cannot win.

unconstitutional: Not allowed by a constitution, which is the highest law of a country or government.

INDEX

WEBSITES

Due to the changing nature of Internet links, PowerKids Press has developed an online list of websites related to the subject of this book. This site is updated regularly. Please use this link to access the list: www.powerkidslinks.com/pltam/cons